SOUTHEND PIER

SOUTHEND PIER

MARTIN EASDOWN

TEMPUS

First published 2007

Tempus Publishing
Cirencester Road, Chalford,
Stroud, Gloucestershire, GL6 8PE
www.tempus-publishing.com

Tempus Publishing is an imprint of NPI Media Group

British Library Cataloguing in Publication Data.
A catalogue record for this book is available from the British Library.

ISBN 978 0 7524 4215 0

Typesetting and origination by NPI Media Group
Printed in Great Britain

Contents

Acknowledgements

The author would like to thank the following for the assistance in the preparation of this book:

Linda Sage; Lynn Tait Gallery; The Southend Pier Museum Foundation; Southend Evening Echo; The National Piers Society and its journal *Piers*.

Introduction

As Sir John Betjeman famously put it, 'The Pier is Southend, Southend is the Pier'. Southend-on-Sea's famous landmark is the longest seaside pleasure pier in the world and has given its town sterling service in times of war and peace. Loved by millions of visitors, Southend Pier is truly one of the icons of the British seaside.

Southend without its pier would seem unthinkable, yet not so long ago there was talk of demolishing it following the disastrous fire of 1976 and the closing of the pier railway two years later. Fortunately, following the support and lobbying of local people and pier lovers such as the great Poet Laureate, the Grade II listed pier was saved, and although seemingly suffering a disaster every ten years or so, its future seems happily assured under the care of Southend Council.

This book does not set out to be a definitive history of the pier; such a history would need to fill a much larger volume than this, but provides an extensive pictorial survey from its inception in 1830 up to 2007.

Further reading on the pier may be found in the titles below:

Southend Pier & its Story 1829-1835-1935 by John William Burrows (author 1936).

The War Story of Southend Pier by A.P. Herbert (County Borough of Southend-on-Sea 1945).

The Story of Southend Pier and its Associations by E.W. Shepherd (Egon Publishers Ltd 1979).

The Longest Pier in the World: A Pictorial History of Southend Pier 1830-1986 by Peggy Dowie & Ken Crowe (The Friends of Southend Pier Museum 1986).

The Longest Pier in the World: A Pictorial History of Southend Pier 1830-1987 (second edition) by Peggy Dowie & Ken Crowe (The Friends of Southend Pier Museum 1987).

A Century of Iron: A History of Southend's Iron Pier 1889-1989 by Peggy Dowie & Ken Crowe (The Friends of Southend Pier Museum 1989).

Southend Pier Railway by K.A. Frost & D.J. Carson (Ian Henry Publications 1990).

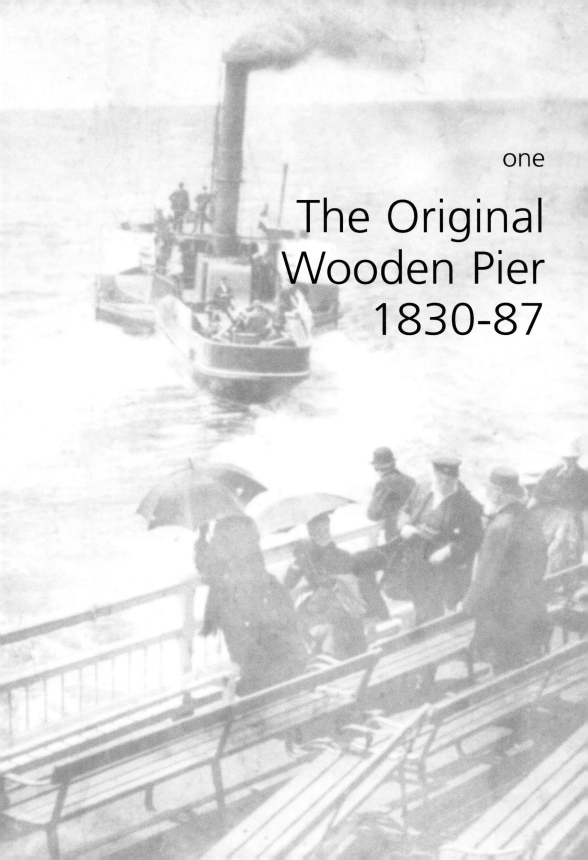

one

The Original
Wooden Pier
1830-87

The Londoner's seaside resort of Southend-on-Sea grew out of a few fishermen's huts situated at the 'south end' of the village of Prittlewell. In 1780 it was a small fishing hamlet of just nineteen houses, yet by this time visitors were coming to stay in the area and hostelries such as the Ship Inn and The Hope were providing accommodation. A theatre was opened in 1793, followed by hot and cold seawater baths two years later. Bathing machines were also available and a daily coach service ran to London. Southend became favoured by the aristocracy with the building of Thomas Holland's 'New Southend' from 1791, which included the *Royal Hotel* and a circulating library. Princess Charlotte came to the resort in 1801 on medical advice for sea bathing, and her mother, Princess Caroline of Brunswick, was a visitor in 1803-4, as was Lady Hamilton in 1803 and 1805.[1]

However, tidal conditions meant that only at extreme high tides could boats disembark passengers at Southend. At other times, visitors had to be either carried or ferried ashore, or use causeways when possible. An early jetty had been erected in 1802 for visitors to the Royal Hotel, and steamers began to call at Southend after 1815, but the idea for a pier was first mooted in 1828 by Alderman William Heygate, a former Lord Mayor of London who lived in Royal Terrace. He was instrumental in the formation of the Southend Pier Company, which had a capital of £12,000 divided into 240 shares of £50 each. The Pier Bill received the Royal Assent on 14 May 1829 and the first pile was driven in on 18 July: seven days later the Lord Mayor of London, Sir William Thompson, laid the foundation stone.

The first 600ft of the pier was opened in June 1830, although it was still too short, except at the lowest tides, to receive vessels that sailed to London, Herne Bay and Margate. A stationary vessel named the *Clarence* (in honour of the Duke of Clarence) was used as the 'pier head' until it was replaced in 1834 by a permanent structure known as the 'Mount'. Nicknamed 'Mount Misery', to reach it at low tide involved a walk or trip on a cart from the pier to a shingle bank, and then a ferry to the Mount.

The Mount soon found itself under attack from marine worms and in order to form a protective layer a coat of nails was hammered into the structure. A new Pier Act in 1835 authorised an extension of the pier to 1,500ft, and a harbour was laid out on the eastern side of the pier. Apparently, however, it was only used by five barges in its first five years: the trading vessels being still run onto the shore at low water and the cargoes loaded into carts.

In 1844 the pier was sold for £17,000 to the chairman of the Eastern Counties Railway, who two years later extended it to 1¼ miles in length, making it the longest pier in Britain. Designed by Messrs Simpson & Lynde and erected by Jonathan Hall, the pier consisted of a 20ft width to a covered area known as the 'Octagon', then progressively narrowed down to 8ft at the sea end. The pier head was 102ft in width and boasted three berthing places for vessels at all states of the tide. A pier head keeper was responsible for maintaining the navigation light at the end of the pier and lived there in a small dwelling.

However, upon its completion (at a cost of £45,000), the pier was ordered to be sold by order of the mortgagees, the Public Works Loan Commissioners. At auction, the pier was purchased by David Waddington for £17,000, who then transferred his interest to Sir Morton Peto, the noted railway contractor who had developed the Cliff Town Estate in the town. Peto passed it on to his business partner Thomas Brassey for £20,000, who later built the railway to Southend in 1856.

The pier acted as a boundary between the boisterous and commercial eastern side of the town and the quieter western side. The opening of the railway brought Southend within easy reach of the people of the East End of London and it became their day trip paradise, although the Cliff Town area managed to retain a somewhat exclusive air. The trippers tended to congregate around the Marine Parade, which became known as the 'Golden Mile'.

With the extension to the pier it was felt necessary to introduce a wooden railway for hand-hauled, or if windy, sail-driven, luggage trucks. Horses were later introduced in 1873 so that passengers could be safely hauled and two years later (upon the pier's acquisition by the Local Board) the wooden rails were re-laid in iron (the horses occasionally caught their hooves in the wooden planking, but a proposal to replace them with elephants was not taken up!). The cost of transporting goods along the pier included: sedan chair 1s 9d; tombstone 5s 3d; harpsichord 2s 6d; corpse £1 1s 0d; turtle 5s 0d and a barrel of red herrings 4d.

The Local Board[2] purchased the pier for £12,000 on 1 July 1875 and as well as upgrading the rails provided a marquee for concerts on the Octagon, manufactured by a local sail maker named Knowles. However, as the tracks ran through the centre of it, all performances had to temporarily cease while the horse tram passed through! A bell rang in the marquee to warn of the approaching tram. However, between 1881 and 1884, the horse tramway was closed due to the unsafe condition of the track.

On 18 January 1881 the pier was cut in two by the barge *West Kent* during a storm. Pier Master Chignell and others were left stranded after they had set out during the gale to bring ashore Pier Head Master Bradley and his family. They were later rescued by boat.

In 1883, a commercial maritime signalling station for Lloyds was placed on the pier head, and two years later the entrance to the pier was graced with an imposing tollhouse, designed by Edward Wright, at a cost of £5,610. The pier itself was by this time badly showing its age and on 29 March 1887 an Act of Parliament was gained to build a new iron pier.

Notes

1. Thomas Holland however had been declared bankrupt in 1797 and his properties were purchased by James Heygate.

2. Southend became a separate parish in 1842 and the Local Board was established in 1866. Prittlewell and Westcliff were absorbed in 1877 and 'Southend-on-Sea' achieved municipal status in 1892, by which time its population numbered 12,000. Extensive residential development led to a large increase in population, which totalled 62,723 in 1911. In 1913 Leigh was taken into the borough and the following year County Borough status was achieved.

An Edwardian postcard captioned 'Southend A.D. 1820', although the pier shown was not built until 1830! This view shows the shore end of the first wooden pier as originally built, along with the Marine Library and a couple of bathing machines sporting Benjamin Beale's modesty hoods. (Marlinova Collection)

Southend Pier around 1840 when 1500ft in length, as depicted by William Henry Bruce. (Marlinova Collection)

A photograph of the wooden pier in 1860, showing the short-lived harbour on the eastern side. (Marlinova Collection/Southend Pier Museum Foundation)

A view of the wooden pier and harbour taken from Pier Hill, c.1860. (Marlinova Collection)

The shore end of the wooden pier in 1864, which now featured two wooden entrance buildings. This postcard was published by J. Adams, Fine Art Depot, Southend-on-Sea, *c.*1910. (Marlinova Collection)

An early photograph of the narrow seaward section of the wooden pier. (Marlinova Collection)

The pier's horse tramway and staff, who sport a mixture of railway- and naval-like uniforms. The horses wear blinkers to keep them on the straight and narrow. (Marlinova Collection/Lynn Tait Gallery)

A watercolour drawing showing the pier after it was damaged by a storm in January 1881. (Marlinova Collection)

Southend Pier in 1882, with a rather ungainly collection of wooden huts lining the shore and a couple of crafts in the harbour. (Marlinova Collection/Lynn Tait Gallery)

The *Lady of Lorne* departing from the wooden pier at Southend, c.1885. (Marlinova Collection)

An 1885 view of Southend Pier, featuring the new entrance building added that year, and the track of the horse tramway. (Marlinova Collection/Lynn Tait Gallery)

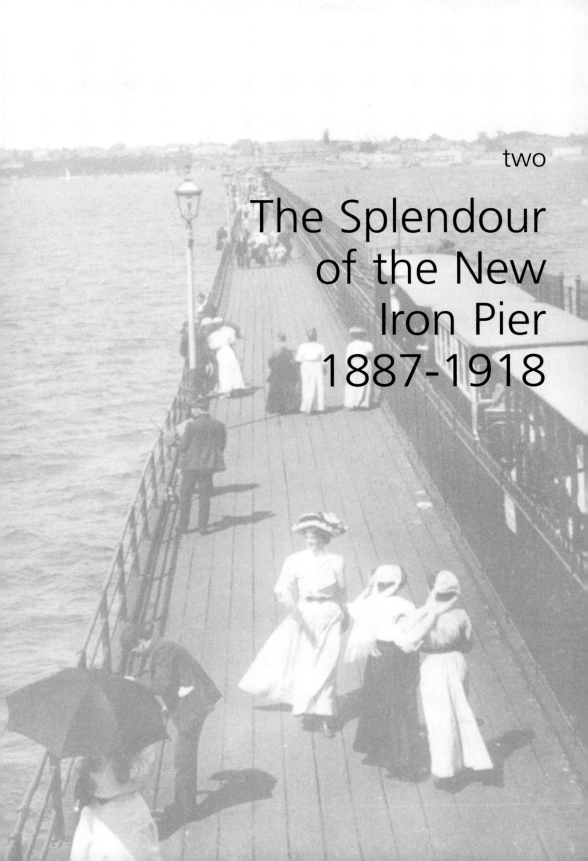

two

The Splendour of the New Iron Pier 1887-1918

The design of noted engineer James Brunlees was chosen for the new pier and the contract to build it was awarded in September 1888 to Messrs Arrol Bros of Glasgow. They quickly proceeded with the work, erecting the pier alongside its wooden predecessor, allowing the first section to be open in July 1889. The main structure was supported on cast-iron screw piles extending 12ft into the foreshore, which were spaced 30ft longitudinally and 9ft laterally. The supports were strengthened with steel tie rods and bracing. To ensure extra stability, a 9ft square grid pattern of supports was added every tenth bay. The timber walkway and rail track were supported on steel joists attached to the main girders. The landing stage was constructed of greenheart piles coated with tar, which were driven 50ft into the clay.

The pier was finally completed in the summer of 1890 and was officially opened on 24 August 1890. At the shore end, a splendid pier pavilion was erected at a cost of £6,643 and a band was formed to perform three times daily during the week. A new electric tramway and generating plant was supplied by Messrs Crompton of Chelmsford and the first 0.75 mile section was opened on 2 August 1890 using a toast-rack car supplied by the Falcon works of Loughborough (the remaining 0.50 miles was opened the following year). A further car was acquired in 1893 and on 28 July 1898 the track acquired a passing loop at a cost of £4,100. Additional cars were ordered in 1902, 1909 and 1914, allowing seven car trains to operate, each seating 250 passengers.

Yet within a few years, steps were taken to extend the pier due to the silting up of the swatch, the main waterway that flowed past the pier head. The son of John Brunlees, James, was retained as engineer (as J. & H. Brunlees) and in March 1896 the tender for constructing the extension was awarded to Messrs Murdoch & Cameron at the cost of £17,191 19s 2d. The slow progress of the work however led to litigation against J. & H. Brunlees and Sir John Wolfe Barry was appointed engineer. The new extension, 450ft in length up to the new pier head, was formally opened in January 1898, in the end having cost £21,000. The length of the pier now measured 7,080ft (1⅓ miles), and between 1893 and 1929 the pier was also progressively widened on its eastern side. The pier was the pride of Southend and between 1892 and the formation of the County Borough in 1914 it was the central feature of the town's coat of arms.

The year 1901 saw a windscreen erected from the tollhouse to the pavilion and a water chute opened adjoining the pier. Although popular, the ride was not allowed to operate on Sundays and was closed in 1905. The basin was then used as a bathing pool and a boating pool before housing the *Golden Hind* replica.

The pier was further improved on 25 July 1908 with the addition on the pier head of a new upper promenade deck with bandstand and covered seating constructed by

Messrs C. Wall & Co. of Grays for £27,950. However, just a few months later, on 3 November 1908, the new pier head was left isolated when the Thames Conservancy hulk *Marlborough* destroyed 60ft of decking. This was the fifth vessel to have hit the new iron pier. In July 1895 two piles were broken when a lighter belonging to the Thames Lighterage Company was carried against the pier in a gale, bringing traffic to a halt for several days, while on 10 December 1898 nearly 100ft of the pier was wrecked when the ketch *Dolphin* was carried through the structure, causing £1,000 worth of damage. There were two further collisions in March and November 1900, and on 7 December 1907 the barge *Robert*, laden with hay, collided with the pier close to the old pier head and broke over a dozen piles, creating a 60ft gap.

The gap between the old and new pier heads was temporarily closed with a suspension bridge until repairs were carried out. However during the following year the pier was damaged again when the barge *Alzima* hit it on 12 July 1909 between the third and fourth shelters, causing damage to the piles.

Fortunately the damage was repaired in time for the visit of the Home and Atlantic Fleets to Southend on 17–25 July 1909. Over 150 ships were anchored off the pier and the ratings were brought ashore in small boats that landed them at the pier head. The pier was heavily patronised during the visit by those who came to view the illuminated ships at night. The structure was also the focus of the town's Yachting Week, and the Royal Yacht *Britannia* was a competitor leading to King George V visiting the pier in 1921 and 1923.

During the First World War the Admiralty took over the pier's signal station, although the pier remained open to the public. In the previous year it had suffered further damage when hit by the barge *Bassildon* 300 yards south of the pavilion: the council received £95 in compensation. Following the end of the war, in September 1919, the German submarine *Deutschland* was exhibited at the pier for ten days on behalf of King George's fund for sailors.

A photograph showing the erection of the iron pier in around 1888 and the temporary wooden gangway to the steamers. In the background can be seen Thompson's Patent Gravity Switchback, erected in 1887. (Marlinova Collection)

A further view of the iron pier under construction, c.1888. (Marlinova Collection)

The new Southend iron pier pictured in 1890. The entrance building was retained from the original wooden pier and was a typical example of florid Victorian design. (Marlinova Collection/ Southend Pier Museum Foundation)

The inaugural run of the pier's new electric toast-rack tram in August 1890. Behind the tram the pier's new pavilion can be seen. (Marlinova Collection/Southend Pier Museum Foundation)

The original pier head on the iron pier showing the lighthouse and a tram on the left of the picture, c.1890. (Marlinova Collection)

An engraving of the Pier Pavilion in the 1890s; built as part of the new iron pier at the cost of £6,463. (Southend Pier Museum Foundation)

The Lord Mayor of London and civic officials proceeding to the Pier Pavilion on Charter Day, 1892. (Marlinova Collection)

The pier entrance and pavilion, c.1900. The elegant kiosk in the foreground sold ices and confectionery. (Marlinova Collection)

Above: In December 1898, the pleasure yacht *Dolphin* was blown into the pier during a strong westerly wind. Around 90ft of the structure was completely wrecked and the vessel sank, fortunately without loss of life. (Marlinova Collection)

Right: A guide to the sailings by the General Steam Navigation Company to Southend, Margate and Ramsgate in the summer of 1902. Fares to Southend from London were 2s single or 3s return. (Marlinova Collection)

Opposite below: The entrance building to the pier, taken from the Hotel Metropole (later the Palace) on 12 December 1900. (Marlinova Collection/Southend Museums)

Below: The pier and water chute photographed from the Hotel Metropole in 1903. This postcard in the IXL Series was posted on 27 February 1904 and was sent to nearby Rayleigh. The Hotel Metropole was soon renamed the Palace Hotel. (Marlinova Collection)

Pier from Hotel Metropole   (Southend-on-Sea)

25

The water chute erected next to the pier in 1901, as featured on a postcard by the Pictorial Stationery Company Peacock Series and posted on 21 May 1904. The ride was not a success however and was dismantled in 1905. (Marlinova Collection)

Local photographer Ellis captures an arctic scene at Southend on 16 January 1905 when the sea froze over. (Marlinova Collection)

A view of the Pier Pavilion taken from the pier, *c.*1905. The pier tramway can also be seen, as can two ladies setting off for a stroll down the long pier neck. (Marlinova Collection)

A rare postcard from around 1905 showing the extension of 1898 before it was substantially improved three years later with the addition of an upper deck. During the day, there was an additional 1*d* toll to walk the extension. (Marlinova Collection)

An Edwardian postcard by the Rotary Photographic Series looking back along the pier from the pier head. (Marlinova Collection)

An unusual postcard showing the sea end train station in 1905, complete with a set of toast-rack trains. (Marlinova Collection)

A postcard by Photocrom Ltd and used on 24 July 1907 showing the *Southend Belle* paddle steamer. The vessel was built in 1896 as part of the famous Belle Steamers fleet of the Coast Development Company. (Marlinova Collection)

The damage to the pier following the collision by the barge *Robert* on 14 December 1907. (Marlinova Collection)

A further postcard view of the damage caused by the *Robert* in 1907. (Marlinova Collection)

The new upper-deck promenade and bandstand on the pier head, opened 25 July 1908. (Marlinova Collection)

The bandstand on the upper level of the new pier extension, pictured in the year of opening, 1908. (Marlinova Collection)

Just a year after the *Robert* disaster, the pier was breached again; this time by the *Marlborough* on 23 November 1908. As a result, the new pier extension was left isolated from the remainder of the pier. (Marlinova Collection)

A further postcard view of the 1908 damage sent on 11 December of that year. The writer comments: 'I thought you would like this p.c. of it, if only for the sake of days gone by. Can you recognise the extension?' (Marlinova Collection)

The suspension bridge temporarily erected over the gap in the pier following the *Marlborough* collision on 23 November 1908. (Marlinova Collection)

A second view of the temporary bridge in 1908, with a group of people happy to pose for the photographer. (Marlinova Collection)

In July 1909 the Home Fleet was reviewed off Southend. This rare postcard shows naval ratings gathered at the pier head. (Marlinova Collection)

The crew of HMS *Queen* afloat off the pier during the Review of the Fleet in July 1909. This unusual postcard was published by Mrs Albert Broom of Fulham. (Marlinova Collection)

HMS *Dreadnought* off Southend Pier as part of the Review of the Fleet in July 1909. This postcard was sent on 26 July and the writer commented that they had suffered stormy weather but the ships were a 'pretty parade'. (Marlinova Collection)

A large crowd has gathered to meet the Lord Mayor as he leaves the pier. (Marlinova Collection)

The toast-rack train at the pier head station on a windy day, c.1910. (Marlinova Collection)

Pier Promenade, Southend-on-Sea.

Above: An unusual view of the pier head taken in 1910 showing a large crowd gathered on the landing stage at the end of the pier. (Marlinova Collection)

Left: The first of a series of postcards of the pier published by G.H. Whittle, who ran a post office at the end of the pier. This postcard view, used on 17 December 1913, is captioned: 'Just a card from the end of the pier a mile and half out at sea.' (Marlinova Collection)

The second Whittle postcard is captioned: 'Sending you this card from the end of the pier 1½ miles out to sea.' The writer mentions he is writing the card on the pier. (Marlinova Collection)

This third postcard by Whittle was sent on the same day as the first card by a person named Cecil. He wrote: 'A mile & half out to sea, fine breezes.' This view shows the pier extension, enlarged in 1908. (Marlinova Collection)

'It's just alright here' writes the sender of the fourth Whittle card, used on 27 May 1913. (Marlinova Collection)

Above: The building of the new pier head station in 1912. New steel rails were introduced at the same time. (Southend Pier Museum Foundation)

Southend Pier Daily, 11.30 and 3.30.

Above: Professor Osbourne also dived off Southend Pier during the Edwardian era; twice daily at 11.30 a.m. and 3.30 p.m. Most pier divers liked to style themselves 'Professors'. Osbourne was also a familiar sight at Southport Pier (the second longest after Southend), where he dived off the tea house roof. (Marlinova Collection)

Right: A programme of the performances of the Pier Orchestral Band on Wednesday, 2 July 1913. Conducted by Adam Seebold, the orchestra gave two performances daily, at 11–12.30 p.m. and 3–5 p.m. The programme also gives details of sailings from the pier by the New Palace Steamers Ltd, the Medway Steam Packet Company and the Belle Steamers. (Marlinova Collection)

Opposite below: The crowd has gathered to watch the lady diver Zetta perform her high-diving act off the pier, *c.*1912. Zetta had a pet duck that used to wait for her in the water! (Marlinova Collection)

'Pier Head, Southend-on-Sea, in the near future' says the caption on this postcard, posted on 22 September 1913. Within a year these superimposed planes and airships would become very much part of the present with their use in the First World War. (Marlinova Collection)

The same photograph, but without the fake aircraft! (Marlinova Collection)

Postmarked in 1914, this view shows promenaders nearing the end of their long walk along the pier. Those who took the toast-rack tram are also nearing the end of their journey. (Marlinova Collection)

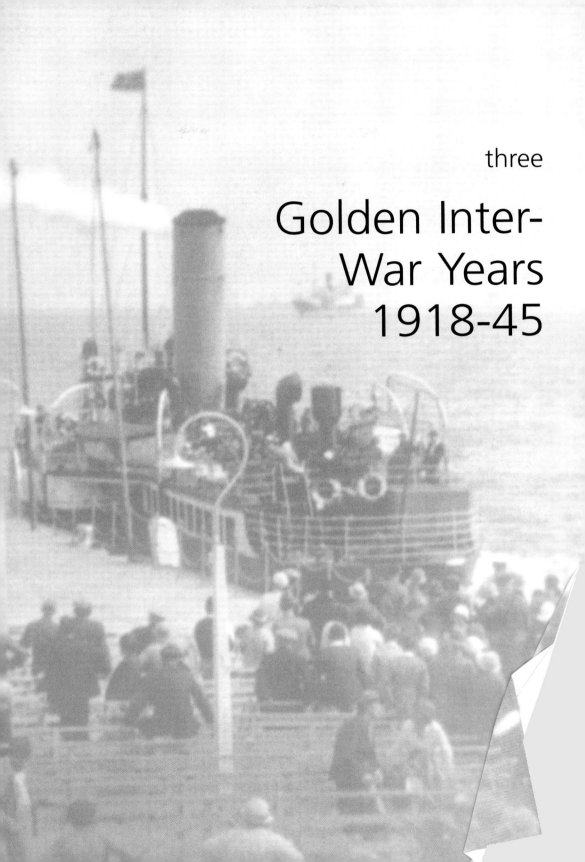

three

Golden Inter-War Years 1918-45

The pier was damaged once again on 18 January 1921 when 160ft of it was destroyed after the concrete motor ship *Violette* broke through between the last shelter and the old pier head. Following the incident red lights were installed along the length of the pier and it was painted with luminous paint. However this failed to prevent the barge *Matilda Upton* being driven through the pier on 17 March 1933, causing a 60ft gap and £20,000 worth of damage. The Council quickly repaired the pier in time for the summer season.

Nevertheless, in spite of these mishaps, the inter-war years saw a number of improvements to the pier, leading to an increase in its usage and popularity. By 1925, visitor numbers had reached over 1.25 million. The pier head was further enlarged in the 1920s, with the main deck measuring 7,640sq. ft and the upper deck 9,000sq. ft. On 8 July 1929, HRH Prince George opened the new berthing arm added on the east side of the pier head, which was named in his honour. Designed by the Borough Engineer and erected by Peter Lind & Co. at a cost of £57,700, the Prince George Extension measured 326ft in length and 30-70ft wide and was constructed using 4,700 tons of reinforced concrete.

The first vessel to use the Prince George Extension was the *Crested Eagle*, which operated on the London-Southend-Margate-Ramsgate route from 1925-32 and then the London-Southend-Clacton-Felixstowe service from 1932-39. She sadly ended her life at Dunkirk in 1940. Before the First World War the famous Belle Steamers plied the East Coast route, sailing from the pier to London, Clacton, Walton, Felixstowe, Southwold, Lowestoft and Great Yarmouth. Sailings to Clacton were also operated by the Eagle and Queen Line, who sailed from Southend to the Kentish resorts of Margate, Herne Bay, Sheerness, the Medway Towns of Rochester and Chatham and occasionally the French coast. Amongst vessels that sailed from the pier were the well-loved *Medway Queen*, *Rochester Queen*, *Royal Sovereign*, *Royal Daffodil* and *Queen of the Channel*. The latter, formerly known as *Woolwich Belle*, ran between Southend and the Medway Towns for Channel Excursions in 1922-32. The *Southend Britannia* provided trips along the local coast.

The beginning of the 1930s saw further improvements to the pier. The old entrance building of 1885 was replaced in 1931 by a higher level access to facilitate a new sea-front road. Two fish motifs were incorporated into brickwork at Prittlewell Priory Park. The tram track was doubled in 1931-32 and three years later a new lifeboat station was opened on the pier head. This was the beneficiary of a legacy from Mr Barclay Harper Walton of London and cost £14,000. The new station was opened in July 1935 by Lord itchie of Dundee and housed the motor lifeboat which arrived at the pier in 1928.

On 18 January 1921 the pier was damaged by the concrete ship *Violette*. This postcard recording the event was issued by the H.C.E. Series using a photograph taken from the *Daily Mail*. (Marlinova Collection)

The pier head was also home to Louis Tussaud's waxworks, which had opened in 1921. This later became the Pier Head Restaurant. The Pier Head Bandstand was home to Adam Seebald and his Pier Orchestra, while in the Pier Pavilion, the 'Bouquets' and the 'Pier Entertainers' (featuring Seebald) held residence throughout the 1930s. A further attraction was added to the pier in 1935 – the illuminations – which by 1955 had fifty-eight set pieces requiring 35,000 lamps.

On 25 August 1939, as Britain prepared to go to war again, the pier was taken over by the Royal Navy as the Thames and Medway Control Headquarters and renamed HMS *Leigh*. Fortified with guns and pill boxes, the pier was attacked by the Luftwaffe on 22 November 1939 but fortunately escaped damage. The pier train was kept running and the pier was used as an assembly point for the armada of small ships that sailed to Dunkirk. The pier performed a vital role as an operations centre for convoys, with some 3,367 vessels sailing from it. The pier was demobilised in 1945 and reopened to the public on 17 May that year.

A side-on view of the *Violette* firmly wedged under the pier. (Marlinova Collection)

An unusual postcard showing the damage to the pier caused by the *Violette*. Note on the right the temporary bridge across the gap. (Marlinova Collection)

A winter toast-rack car, pictured in 1922. (Marlinova Collection/Southend Pier Museum Foundation)

The boating pool beside the pier (on the site of the old water chute) pictured on a postcard sent in 1923. Interestingly, the back of the postcard advertises London pools at Forest Gate, Clapton, Catford, Hammersmith, Tooting Bec and Clapham Common. (Marlinova Collection)

THE LONGEST PIER IN ENGLAND, SOUTHEND-ON-SEA   Nº 33.

Above: The longest pier in England, photographed in 1924. The boating pool looks very quiet! (Marlinova Collection)

Left: A very rare postcard, published by The Locomotive Publishing Company Ltd, showing the Prince George Extension under construction. The writer of the card has written: 'Good Friday 1928 – driving piles for new steamer landing stage, Southend Pier.' (Marlinova Collection)

A further view of the pile driving of the new Prince George Extension on Good Friday 1928. (Marlinova Collection)

The Prince George Extension was opened on 8 July 1929 and this postcard shows it as originally built, bedecked with flags. (Marlinova Collection)

A later view of the Prince George Extension in the 1930s with the upper deck having been added to the structure. (Marlinova Collection)

A steamer departs from the Prince George Extension, c.1930. (Marlinova Collection/Southend Pier Museum Foundation)

A view along the pier taken from the Prince George Extension in 1934. (Marlinova Collection)

The art-deco influenced entrance to the pier opened in 1931. (Marlinova Collection)

Southend Pier in 1931 with the Pier Pavilion advertising its fun fair and café. (Marlinova Collection)

A postcard showing the damage caused to the pier by the barge *Matilda Upton* on 17 March 1933. (Marlinova Collection)

The pier undergoing repairs with the assistance of the vessel *Prittlewell*. (Marlinova Collection)

'The Gateway to Happiness' claims the cover of this guide for the pier and pavilion for the 1933 season. (Marlinova Collection)

County Borough of Southend-on-Sea.

SOUTHEND PIER.

Season. 1933.

Programme of Performances
BY THE
Pier Orchestral Band.

CONDUCTOR : MR. ADAM SEEBOLD.
Leader : Mr. PHILLIP LA RIVIERE.

Left: A page in the 1933 guide advertising the Pier Orchestra performances, conducted by Adam Seebold. There were three performances daily. (Marlinova Collection)

Below: Adam Seebold and his orchestra, who performed at the pier head throughout the 1930s. Seebold had begun his career on the pier before the First World War. (Southend Pier Museum Foundation)

Another page in the 1933 guide highlighting the attractions in the Pier Pavilion (Palais de Danse) and the Pier Head Bandstand. (Marlinova Collection)

The Queen Line Steamers sailing from Southend Pier in 1933, with journeys available to France, the Kent coast and the East Coast. (Marlinova Collection)

The pier by night featured on a postcard in the Excel Series and was posted on 23 July 1934. (Marlinova Collection)

A postcard view of the pier by Valentines photographed from the bottom of Pier Hill in 1935. The pier is advertising Southend's Yachting Week. (Marlinova Collection)

The official opening of the Southend Pier lifeboat station in July 1935. (Marlinova Collection)

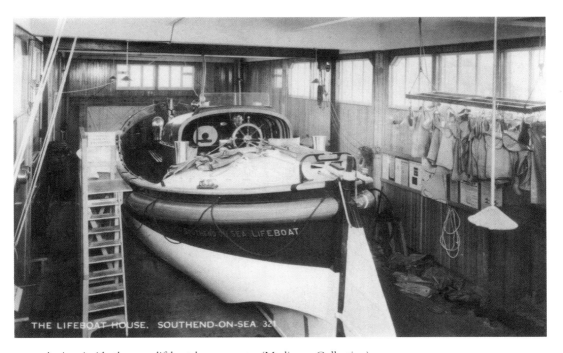

A view inside the new lifeboat house, c.1935. (Marlinova Collection)

A postcard depicting the pier's centenary in 1935, although in reality it was 105 years old. The 1835 date refers to when the pier was first placed on Admiralty charts. (Marlinova Collection)

The toast-rack train on Southend Pier just leaving the station under the pavilion during the 1930s. (Marlinova Collection)

An aerial view by Photocrom showing the pier head during the 1930s. (Marlinova Collection)

A fine view by Lansdowne of the pier head taken during the 1930s, featuring the paddle steamer *Royal Eagle*. Note the welcome lettering on the pier 'Southend-on-Sea for Health and Pleasure'. (Marlinova Collection)

The Pier Bandstand pictured during the 1930s. (Marlinova Collection)

The Pier Entertainers for the 1935 season. (Marlinova Collection)

The pier and lifeboat house pictured from the upper deck of the pier head during the 1930s. (Marlinova Collection)

A postcard showing the *Golden Eagle* at the pier head during the 1930s. (Marlinova Collection)

Above: A view looking back to the old pier head from the upper deck of the extension in the 1930s. (Marlinova Collection)

Left: Upon the outbreak of the Second World War, the pier was closed to the public and was taken over by the Admiralty and renamed HMS *Leigh*. (Southend Pier Museum Foundation)

Scenes on the pier during the war, taken from the book *The War Story of Southend Pier* by A.P. Herbert, featuring the anti-aircraft guns placed on the pier head. Mr Herbert recommended that the pier deserved a George Cross for its wartime service. (from the book *The War Story of Southend Pier*)

four

Post-War Boom then Bust 1945-80

The immediate post-war years were a boom time for the pier, with over 3.3 million people using the railway in 1947. With the old trains struggling to cope, the Council decided to introduce new enclosed electric trains for the 1949 season, manufactured by A.C. Cars Ltd of Middlesex at a cost of £99,100. That year proved to be a watershed in the pier's popularity: the new trains carried 4.5 million visitors, while another million walked the pier. The new trains were kept busy throughout the 1950s as the pier continued to be a favoured attraction. Ben Oakley and his Orchestra attracted great crowds to the Pier Head Sun Deck Theatre, while the Pier Pavilion hosted the popular summer shows such as 'Zip-a-Hoy' and 'Out of the Blue'. The pier head was also home to a games deck, hall of mirrors, restaurants (including the Dolphin, erected in 1950 from scrap metal and timber left by the Royal Navy), a radar school and a Lloyd's shipping office on the Prince George Extension.

Sadly the Pier Pavilion was destroyed by fire on 6 October 1959, although fortunately the prompt action of the Pier Master Mr Goble in driving away the trains saved them from also being incinerated. Five hundred people were left stranded at the pier head because of the fire and they made their escape by climbing down steps to the boulevard or onto boats. The pavilion was replaced by a ten-pin bowling centre in 1962.

However, by the early 1960s both visitor numbers and calling pleasure craft were in decline as Southend experienced a downward spiral of paying guests (although day visitor numbers remained respectable).[1] The last visit of the popular steamer *Medway Queen* was in September 1963 and by the end of the decade annual visitors had fallen to one million. The revenue lost had led to the pier becoming a heavy financial burden on the Council and in 1970 they decided it should be leased out to a private firm for a fixed annual sum of £25,000 and a proportion of the profits. Nevertheless the rumblings continued about the financial burden the pier placed on the local taxpayer. There were calls for its demolition, and although the Council denied this would happen, the pier railway was reduced to a single track in 1973. Three years later work began on a planned £3 million five-year repair programme, but that was stopped in its tracks by a disastrous fire on 29 July 1976 which totally destroyed the pier head. Strong winds and a lack of water due to a very low tide meant that the blaze had soon taken hold, in spite of the best efforts of tugs from across the river in Kent and local crop sprayer Laddi Marmol flying his plane over the pier and dropping 400 gallons of water (he later re-enacted it for the first Pier Festival in 1980). Around 500 people trapped on the pier were ferried to safety.

The damage amounted to £1.4 million, from which only £408,000 was recoverable from insurance (leading to the Council being unable to afford to insure the pier). The

A photograph taken by G.A. Osborn of the well-loved paddle steamer *Medway Queen* at Southend Pier on 12 August 1948. The vessel was built in 1924 and usually ran between the Medway Towns and Southend. She was withdrawn in 1963 and after becoming derelict a fight began to save her, which at last looks like it may succeed. (Marlinova Collection)

situation continued to go from bad to worse: the bowling alley was damaged by a fire in November 1977 to the tune of £200,000 and then in October 1978 the pier railway was closed after it was declared to be unsafe, resulting in a large drop in visitors. A 'Save Southend Pier' action group was formed and received the support of pier lover Sir John Betjeman, who uttered his immortal words 'The Pier is Southend, Southend is the Pier.' The plight of Southend Pier, along with those at Clevedon, Bangor and Brighton, led to the formation of the National Piers Society in 1979, where first the president was John Betjeman.

In mid-1979, the action group were informed by the Council that the pier's lease was available for £700,000 and if there were no takers by 1 March 1980 demolition of the structure would be considered. When no offers were received, the deadline was extended to September, but still no one came forward so on 1 August the Council announced they were to close the pier at the end of September. Fortunately, on 20 September it was announced that the pier's amusement company, Lecorgne Amusements (who had run an amusement arcade on the pier since 1964), would run the pier on a trial basis until a long-term solution was found.

Note

1. Southend successfully reinvented itself, however, as a regional centre for shopping and industry.

Left: A programme for Wednesday, 15 September 1948 advertising performances of Ben Oakley and his Orchestra at the Pier Head Bandstand. The Pier Pavilion was hosting the popular holiday show *Bubbles.* (Marlinova Collection)

Below: A photograph taken on 15 January 1949 showing one of the pier's toast-rack trains that were shortly to be withdrawn from service. (Marlinova Collection)

Opposite above: The old tank car of the Southend Pier Railway, photographed on 15 January 1949. (Marlinova Collection)

Opposite below: The old and new in 1949: a toast rack pictured with one of its successors. (Marlinova Collection)

Above: One of the four new electric trains introduced onto the pier in 1949. (Marlinova collection)

Below: Launching the lifeboat from the boathouse on Southend Pier, *c.*1950. (Marlinova Collection)

LAUNCHING THE SOUTHEND-ON-SEA LIFEBOAT. 323

Right: A programme of Eagle and Queen Line steamer services from Southend Pier in 1952. Sailings included the *Royal Daffodil* to Margate and the French coast, *Rochester Queen* to Herne Bay, *Medway Queen* to Sheerness and the Medway Towns, *Queen of the Channel* to Clacton, *Royal Sovereign* and the *Crested Eagle* to Margate and Ramsgate. (Marlinova Collection)

Below: A 1950s aerial view of the longest pier in the world featuring a vessel steaming away from the pier head. (Marlinova Collection)

SOUTHEND PIER — LONGEST IN THE WORLD

Photograph by Hubert Thompson, A.R.P.S.

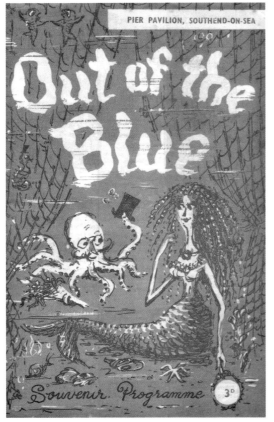

Above: The pier train on a quiet day in the 1950s. (Marlinova Collection)

Left: A programme for the 1956 production in the Pier Pavilion of the popular show *Out of the Blue*. (Marlinova Collection)

Above: An unusual view of the pier head, taken from the sea during the 1950s. (Marlinova Collection)

Right: A flyer advertising Queen Line sailings from Strood Pier to Southend, Herne Bay and Clacton in June 1957. Trains to Maidstone from Strood connected with the sailings. (Marlinova Collection)

QUEEN LINE of STEAMERS
(THE NEW MEDWAY STEAM PACKET CO., LTD.)

COMBINED
RAIL and STEAMER TICKETS
From SAT., 8th JUNE
to 15th SEPT., 1957

TO

SOUTHEND
EVERY DAY
(Excepting Fridays & 22nd June)

HERNE BAY
SUNDAYS, MONDAYS
WEDNESDAYS & THURSDAYS

CLACTON
NEW THROUGH SERVICE EVERY SATURDAY
(Excepting 22nd June) and TUESDAY

Combined Rail (2nd Class) and Steamer Fares by any Train to connect with Steamer at Strood

FROM	Convenient Connecting Train Services			Southend Day Return	Herne Bay Day Return	Clacton Day Return
	Week'd's	Sundays				
		June 9 & 16	June 23 to Sep.15			
				s. d.	s. d.	s. d.
MAIDSTONE W.	8.07	8.07	8.27	10/9	12/9	14/3
MAIDSTONE Bks.	8.08	8.08	8.28	10/6	12/6	14/-
AYLESFORD	8.13	8.13	8.33	10/-	12/-	13/6
NEW HYTHE ...	8.16	8.16	8.36	9/11	11/11	13/5
SNODLAND ...	8.19	8.19	8.39	9/8	11/8	13/2
HALLING ...	8.22	8.22	8.42	9/5	11/5	12/11
CUXTON ...	8.25	8.25	8.45	8/10	10/10	12/4

Passengers should enquire whether the above train times will operate at Bank Holiday periods

Children 3 and under 14 years of age half fares

Steamer leaves **STROOD PIER** at 9 a.m.
Depart **CLACTON** 4.25 p.m.: **HERNE BAY** 5.00 p.m., **SOUTHEND** 6.40 p.m.
Convenient Trains from STROOD to MAIDSTONE and intermediate stations after arrival of Steamer.

EXCELLENT CATERING & STEAMERS FULLY LICENSED

Passengers are carried only on the Terms and Conditions printed in the British Transport Commission's Publications and Notices and those of the New Medway Steam Packet Co., Ltd., printed on the back of this handbill.

All Sailings subject to Weather and Other Circumstances Permitting

Further Information and Tickets can be obtained at:
British Railways Southern Region Stations and Booking Offices or
Steamer Office, Strood Pier

QUEEN LINE HEAD OFFICE, 385-7 HIGH ST., ROCHESTER.
Phone : CHATHAM 2204-5

No.1   W-46/5-57/5m./20005.   K.A.P. Ltd.

A postcard of the pier and *Golden Hind* replica sent on 21 June 1958, on which the young writer has written: 'At the moment we are eating ices at the end of Southend Pier. The pier is a mile long, 6*d* for me and 1*s* for mummy and daddy.' (Marlinova Collection)

A busy day on the pier extension during the 1950s. (Marlinova Collection)

The *Golden Hind* replica at the shore end of the pier in the 1950s. The popular show *Bubbles* is the feature in the Pier Pavilion. (Marlinova Collection)

The pier train passing promenaders returning from the pier head, *c.*1960. (Marlinova Collection)

Left: A feature of the pier for a number of years during the 1950s and 1960s was Jerry Jerome's 'Zip-a-Hoy' staged at the Pier Head Sun Deck Theatre. (Marlinova Collection)

Below: The electric trains on the pier seen from the seaward station, *c.*1960. (Marlinova Collection)

Opposite: A fully decorated pier head complete with two swans, *c.*1960. (Marlinova Collection/Southend Pier Museum Foundation)

The illuminated shore end of the pier in the early 1960s photographed before the erection of the bowling alley in 1963. (Marlinova Collection)

Opposite above: A further view of the illuminations, which extol visitors to walk to the pier head. (Marlinova Collection)

Opposite below: The pier in the early 1960s, featuring the new bowling centre erected in 1962 on the site of the old pavilion. (Marlinova Collection)

VISIT THE PIER HEAD

The Pier, Southend-on-Sea   40551

The pier photographed during the summer of 1975. (Marlinova Collection)

A photograph of the pier train in 1975. (Marlinova Collection)

YOU ARE AT THE END OF THE *LONGEST* PIER IN THE WORLD

The pier head in 1975. Twelve months later all would be destroyed in the great blaze of July 1976. (Marlinova Collection)

Above: A further view of the soon-to-be destroyed pier-head buildings in 1975. (Marlinova Collection)

Left: A view of the pier taken from the top of the pier-head buildings in 1975. (Marlinova Collection)

Looking along the long walkway of Southend Pier in 1975. (Marlinova Collection)

The Pavilion Lanes Bowling Centre pictured in 1975. (Marlinova Collection)

S·O·S PIER FIRE
JULY 1976

A fireman damps down the lower deck of the pier following the 1976 fire; photographed by Lecorgne's Amusements. (Marlinova Collection)

Opposite above: An aerial view of the disastrous fire that destroyed the pier head on 4 July 1976. Two tugs are desperately trying to fight the fire. (Marlinova Collection/Southend Pier Museum Foundation)

Opposite below: Another aerial view of the 1976 fire, part of a set issued by Lecorgne's Amusements Ltd situated on the pier head. (Marlinova Collection)

The devastating scene at the end of the world's longest pleasure pier in 1976, once again captured by Lecorgne's Amusements. (Marlinova Collection)

The burnt-out skeletal frame of the pier head, photographed by Lecorgnes after the 1976 fire. (Marlinova Collection)

A closer view of the carnage wrought by the fire, once more captured by Lecorgnes. (Marlinova Collection)

The programme of events for the Southend Pier Festival held over the weekend of 27 and 28 September 1980. (Marlinova Collection)

The 'Save our Pier' campaign in 1980 when Southend Borough Council threatened to close the pier. (Marlinova Collection)

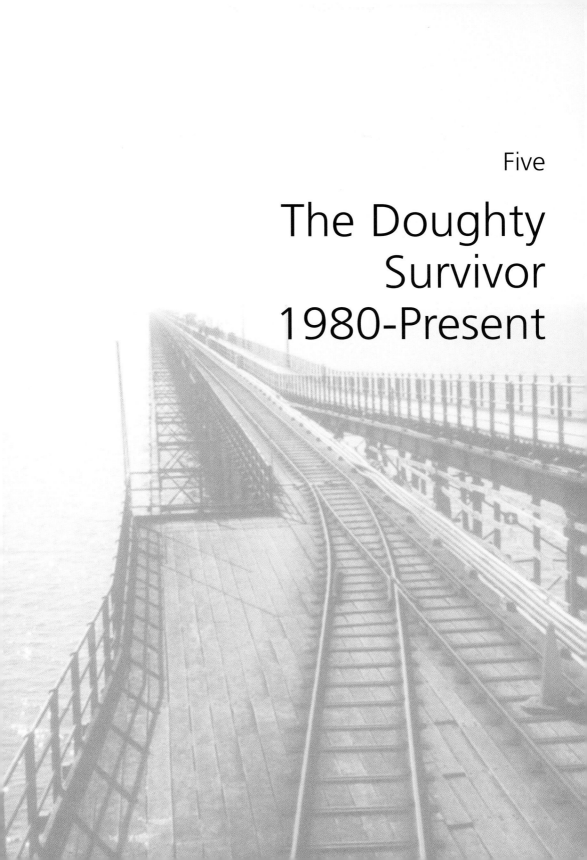

Five

The Doughty
Survivor
1980-Present

Lecorgnes took over the running of the pier from 1 October 1980, although the pier trains remained dormant. In 1982 they were taken away for scrap, although some survived and two were later purchased for the Pier Museum. However the future of the pier looked a lot rosier in 1983 when it was announced that a £1 million refurbishment (£800,000 million from the Council, £200,000 million from the Government's Historic Buildings Committee) would commence in November 1984, which would include restoration of the pier railway with two new diesel operated trains on a 3ft gauge single track with passing loop. The new trains were built by Messrs Severn-Lamb Ltd of Stratford-upon-Avon and were each comprised of five aluminium bodies on steel frames. They were officially named after two staunch supporters of the pier *Sir William Heygate* and *Sir John Betjeman*. The railway was officially opened by Princess Anne on 2 May 1986, who took the twelve-minute journey to the pier head. The final cost of the refurbishment of the pier was £1.3 million, of which £223,627 was spent on the new railway.

Unfortunately, just one month later, the pier suffered another of its mishaps when the 180ft vessel *Kingsabbey* sliced through the walkway leading to the pier head on 30 June 1986. £500,000 worth of damage was sustained, which included a 70ft gap in the pier and the destruction of the lifeboat station. An ex-railway footbridge was used to temporarily bridge the gap before the Council carried out repairs at a cost of £115,586. The captain of the *Kingsabbey* was fined £1,000 for not being present on the bridge at the time of the collision.

Between 1986 and 1988 the pier was managed by Brent-Walker, whose plans to erect new leisure buildings on the pier failed to materialise. The centenary of the iron pier in 1989 saw new toilets and a café erected on the stem extension and the establishment of a pier museum underneath the shore-end station. The museum, which is run by a charitable trust and staffed by volunteers, is open four days a week between May and October. Amongst the many interesting and historic artefacts are restored carriages from the pier railway and a working signal box.

In January 1991 Princess Anne returned to the pier to open the new lifeboat station on the Prince George Extension. The following year saw the announcement of a £1.5 million development of the pier head in partnership with the Stockvale Company, proprietors of the Peter Pan's Playground on the shore by the pier. A Victorian-styled pavilion was envisaged housing a restaurant, bar, food court, shops, performance stage, family entertainment area and covered walkway from the pier head station. However the project was shelved because of the cost.

The ten-year cycle of disasters to the pier continued in 1995 with the destruction of the bowling alley pavilion by fire on 7 June. The pier railway beneath the building suffered some damage but was repaired. AMF Bowling, who had operated the pavilion, announced their wish to rebuild it in spite of a new ten-pin bowling centre planned for the revamped Kursaal. This led to the Council getting cold feet to replace the pier bowling centre and in the year 2000 announced their intention to build either a replica of the 1890 pavilion (destroyed by fire in 1959) or a modern one constructed of crystal. However, in 2007, the site remains empty.

Meanwhile, the pier head gained an open-air pavilion with a small stage and shops in 1997, much to the disappointment of many who disliked its lightweight construction. It was certainly a step down from the plans given the go ahead the previous year for a modernist building, incorporating a 'wave-like' roof and an arcade area with traditional seaside arts and crafts, photographic studio, palmistry, souvenirs, ice cream parlour and catering outlet.

A much more favourable development took place in 2002 with the addition of a high-level sundeck over the RNLI station. A new water main and sewage-disposal system was also installed, as were new fire hydrants and improved illuminations. In July 2002, work began on restoring the area still bearing the scars of the 1976 fire. Funded by the Council at a cost of £2.5 million, the work also included a general overhaul of the structure of the pier. Re-measurement of the pier that year recorded a length of 7,293ft (1.38 miles).

Further improvements to the pier were carried out in 2003 with the building of a new entrance and bridge across the sea-front road, giving disabled access to the pier from the High Street via a new lift. The designers, Peter Emptage Associates Ltd, gained the RIBA East Spirit of Integrity Architectural Award for the work. The £1.9 million cost was funded by Europe as part of the Southend Seafront, High Street & Pier Enhancement Project (SSHAPE). The town's tourist information centre was relocated in the pier entrance.

Sadly, the ten-year curse of misfortune struck the pier again, when on Sunday, 9 October 2005, at around 10.40 p.m., a fire broke out at McGinty's pub at the end of the pier. Firemen fought the blaze throughout the night, yet the pub, pier head railway station, amusement arcade, café and souvenir shop (covering an area of 130ft) were all destroyed.

Nevertheless, the trains were soon running down the pier again, to a temporary halt adjoining the burnt-out shell of the pier head station. The pier trains received a new blue and cream livery (matching that of Southend's buses) and the unloved open-air pavilion was demolished, leading to a smartening up of the end of the pier with new seating and lighting. A new pier head café was opened in time for the 2007 season.

In 2007 the pier deservedly won the National Piers Society's 'Pier of the Year' award, with NPS President Gavin Henderson observing: 'The heroic survival through fire and tempest of our longest and most possibly tenacious pier makes it fully deserving of its accolade.' Commenting on the award, Southend Council's Anne Holland summed up the pier's everlasting appeal: 'It is the heart of Southend and is an icon much loved by the town's residents.'

A 1986 view of the pier taken by the Lynn Tait Gallery (Marlinova Collection)

One of the two new pier trains introduced in 1986. (Marlinova Collection)

The pier train *Sir John Betjeman* in the shore end station in 1986. (Marlinova Collection/Lynn Tait Gallery)

The unveiling of the plaque by HRH Princess Anne commemorating the inauguration of the new train service on Southend Pier in 1986. (Marlinova Collection/Lynn Tait Gallery)

In addition to opening the new train service, Her Royal Highness also dedicated the lifeboat *Percy Garon II*. (Marlinova Collection/Lynn Tait Gallery)

Just weeks after Princess Anne's visit, the pier was cut in two by the motor tanker *Kingsabbey* on 30 June 1986. (Marlinova Collection/Lynn Tait Gallery)

The moment when the *Kingsabbey* sliced through the lifeboat slipway. (Marlinova Collection/Lynn Tait Gallery)

A view of the broken pier deck and lifeboat slipway following the *Kingsabbey* collision. The lifeboat station was declared unsafe and demolished, and a new one was erected on the Prince George Extension. (Marlinova Collection/Lynn Tait Gallery)

A close-up view of the gap in the pier left by the *Kingsabbey* on 30 June 1986. (Marlinova Collection/Lynn Tait Gallery)

The Southend Pier train is featured on a publicity postcard issued by Southend-on-Sea Borough Council. (Marlinova Collection)

The entrance to Southend Pier in January 1987 following a heavy fall of snow. The card was sent by Lynn Tait to the late Nova Saunders, a pier postcard enthusiast (and the 'nova' in 'Marlinova'). (Marlinova Collection/Lynn Tait Gallery)

Southend Pier illuminated in 1988. (Marlinova Collection/Lynn Tait Gallery)

The first day cover commemorating the centenary of the iron pier in 1989. (Marlinova Collection)

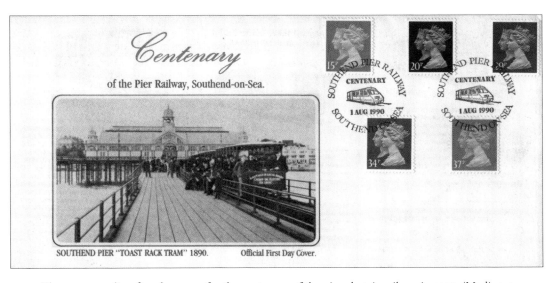

The corresponding first day cover for the centenary of the pier electric railway in 1990. (Marlinova Collection)

Opposite above: A band plays on the pier during the centenary celebrations in 1989. (Marlinova Collection)

Opposite below: The young girl seems unimpressed with the man on the stilts during the centenary celebrations in 1989! (Marlinova Collection)

The entrance to Southend Pier photographed in October 1990. (Marlinova Collection)

Looking along a deserted pier deck on a blustery autumn day in October 1990. (Marlinova Collection)

A view looking towards the Prince George Extension in October 1990. (Marlinova Collection)

The deserted buildings at the end of the pier in October 1990. (Marlinova Collection)

Certificate

This is to Certify that the person named below did walk the length of Southend Pier

One and One Third Miles (approx)

(and he was well knackered at the end of it!)

Name *Martin Easdown*

Date *30th October 1990*

A certificate purchased by the author on 30 October 1990 to commemorate his walk to the end of the pier! (Marlinova Collection)

The Princess Royal returned to the pier on 24 January 1991 to open the new lifeboat house on the Prince George Extension. (Marlinova Collection/Lynn Tait Gallery)

A postcard published in the early 1990s by the Alternative Co. Ltd, Pier Emporium featuring the *Sir John Betjeman* train at the pier head station. (Marlinova Collection)

Southend-On-Sea
Home Of The World's Longest Pier

Three fire appliances, two from Southend and one from Shoebury, fought the blaze, which totally destroyed the building. (Marlinova Collection/Lynn Tait Gallery)

Opposite above: A group of promenaders watch the pier train on a sunny day in the early 1990s. The white building in the background is the old Palace Hotel, opened as the Hotel Metropole in 1904. (Marlinova Collection)

Opposite below: On Wednesday, 7 June 1995 the pier bowling alley was burnt down, continuing the ten-year cycle of disasters afflicting the pier. This view was photographed at 9.05 a.m. by John Lidstone for the Lynn Tait Gallery. (Marlinova Collection/Lynn Tait Gallery)

A photograph of the pier shortly after the fire taken from Pier Hill. (Marlinova Collection)

Opposite above: Following the collapse of the pavilion floor, the fire spread to the railway station underneath. The fire fighters were forced to fight the blaze in the confined area of radiated heat using breathing apparatus. (Marlinova Collection/Lynn Tait Gallery)

Opposite below: The aftermath of the 1995 fire, with a few wisps of smoke still emanating from the charred metalwork. (Marlinova Collection/Southend Pier Museum Foundation)

The PIER

The Newsletter of Southend Pier Museum Foundation

Chairman

Peggy Dowie
36 Shaftesbury Avenue
Thorpe Bay
Tel. 614553

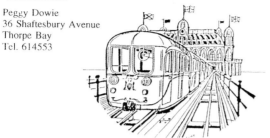

SEPTEMBER 1997

SEE INSIDE FOR DETAILS OF **TWO** GREAT DAYS OUT.

Left: The September 1997 cover of *The Pier*, the newsletter of the Southend Pier Museum Foundation, led by that redoubtable protector of the pier, Peggy Dowie. (Marlinova Collection)

Below: The shore end of the pier photographed in September 1998. The site of the burnt-out bowling pavilion has still to be redeveloped. (Marlinova Collection)

The charred timber of the 1976 fire could still be seen twelve years later in September 1998. (Marlinova Collection)

The much-criticised new open-air pavilion, erected on the pier head in 1997, photographed in September 1998. Small retail units and a café surrounded the open performance area. (Marlinova Collection)

The fenced-off area of the old bowling pavilion, seen in September 1998. (Marlinova Collection)

PLEASURE ON THE PIER 2000

SOUTHEND PIER

Events 2000 on the longest pleasure pier in the world

July and August
Visit Southend's Chelsea Flower Show display on the Pier Walkway

Sunday 16th July 2000
First Annual Southend Pier Charity Crabbing Competition

Sunday 30th July 2000 & Sunday 6th August 2000
Ponjo's Hot Four Lunchtime Jazz on the Walkway (Shore End)

Tuesday 1st August 10am - 1pm   Bizz Angling Courses
Wednesday 2nd August 10am - 1pm   for over 10 year olds
Thursday 3rd August 11am - 2pm   With Dave Godwin
                        AND
Tuesday 15th August 10am - 1pm   More Bizz Angling Courses
Wednesday 16th August 10.30am - 1.30pm for over 10 year olds
Thursday 17th August 11am - 2pm

Thursday, Friday, Saturday & Sunday 10th, 11th, 12th & 13th August 2000
Grand Puppet Festival

Saturday 26th August 2000
Southend Annual Barge Match

Saturday & Sunday 26th & 27th August 2000
Nigel the Clown

Saturday & Sunday 2nd & 3rd September 2000
Southend Water Festival

Saturday & Sunday 16th & 17th September 2000
International Clowns Jamboree

'The Pleasure on the Pier' during the summer of 2000 which included a flower show, lunchtime jazz, angling and crabbing competitions, puppets and clowns and the Southend Annual Barge Match and Water Festival. (Marlinova Collection)

The Radio Caroline vessel docked at the pier head on a wet day in August 1999. (Marlinova Collection)

A surviving pier toast-rack train on display in the Southend Pier Museum. Between its withdrawal from service in 1949 and 1987 it was used as a chicken shed by a farmer in Benfleet before it was retrieved and restored by the Southend Pier Museum Foundation. (Marlinova Collection/ Southend Pier Museum Foundation)

The pier head photographed in July 2001, featuring the new RNLI station visible on the Prince George Extension. (Marlinova Collection)

Van Looy's restaurant at the end of the pier, taken in July 2001. Their speciality was fresh, local fish 'battered by experts'. In the following year the restaurant was renamed 'Marriotts'. (Marlinova Collection)

VAN LOOY'S
PIER HEAD
FISH & CHIPS
(NFFF)

65 SEATER RESTAURANT

FRESH LOCAL FISH

SOUTHEND PIER

BATTERED BY EXPERTS

COACH PARTIES WELCOME

KIDS MENU   BURGERS
SALADS   SNACKS
ALL DAY BREAKFAST

PHONE:
01702 616163/613210
SEA VIEWS

EPS Printing Ltd · 01702 391676

A flyer for Van Looy's pier head fish and chip restaurant, where the author enjoyed a good meal in July 2001. (Marlinova Collection)

The pier head buildings in July 2001, featuring the Emporium gift shop, post box and Van Looy's restaurant on the left and McGinty's bar and café on the right. With the exception of Van Looy's, all these buildings would be destroyed in the fire of October 2005. (Marlinova Collection)

The pier train *Sir John Betjeman* heading towards the shore in July 2001. (Marlinova Collection)

The site of the former bowling alley in July 2001, now just a bare deck of wood. (Marlinova Collection)

Looking towards the shore from the pier, July 2001. (Marlinova Collection)

The upper promenade deck at the shore end of the pier, known as 'Promenade Way'. The photograph was taken in July 2002, during the Southend Pier Heritage Festival. (Marlinova Collection)

The restored toast rack No.8 on show on the Promenade Way in July 2002. (Marlinova Collection)

The popular Southend song duo Pier Talk (Chris Jones and Jack Forbes) perform for the author during the Southend Pier Heritage Festival in July 2002. (Marlinova Collection)

The shore end of the pier in July 2002. (Marlinova Collection)

Punch and Judy on the pier during the Southend Pier Heritage Festival, July 2002. This area was totally destroyed in the 2005 fire. (Marlinova Collection)

The pavilion on the pier pictured in July 2002. (Marlinova Collection)

The small stage provided within the pavilion, July 2002. (Marlinova Collection)

The RNLI station on the Prince George Extension, opened in January 1991 and seen here in July 2002. (Marlinova Collection)

The upper deck of the RNLI station, an attractive seating area, photographed in July 2002.
(Marlinova Collection)

Seen at the pier head in July 2002, the river-going paddle steamer *Kingswear Castle* operates a
popular summer service between Southend and the Medway Towns. The PS *Waverley* and MV
Balmoral are also callers at the pier. (Marlinova Collection)

Looking down from the upper deck of the RNLI station towards the pavilion in July 2002. Note the burnt-out area of decking remaining from the 1976 fire. (Marlinova Collection)

The old pier head buildings in July 2003, featuring the Emporium gift shop and Marriott's refreshment rooms. (Marlinova Collection)

Looking along the pier from the RNLI station in July 2003, whilst re-decking work is in progress. (Marlinova Collection)

The new entrance to the pier, photographed in the year that it opened, 2003. (Marlinova Collection)

A closer view of the burnt-out sea-end train station in October 2005. (Courtesy of *Southend Evening Echo*)

Opposite above: Almost thirty years on from the devastating conflagration of 1976, the pier head was ravaged by fire once again during the night of 9-10 October 2005. (Courtesy of *Southend Evening Echo*)

Opposite below: The aftermath of the 2005 blaze the following morning, showing the smouldering skeletal remains of the pier head station and the adjoining buildings. (Courtesy of *Southend Evening Echo*)

Fire fighters damp down the dying embers of the fire at the pier head station in October 2005. (Courtesy of *Southend Evening Echo*)

Opposite above: The revamped entrance to the pier taken from the new pier hill lift in January 2006. (Marlinova Collection)

Opposite below: The pier railway's single-car unit (acquired in 1996) at the temporary pier head station in January 2006. (Marlinova Collection)

The fire-destroyed pier head station, photographed in January 2006. (Marlinova Collection)

The promenade and railway decks seen from the widened shore end of the pier in March 2007. (Marlinova Collection)

The single-unit car trundling down the pier at the passing loop in March 2007. (Marlinova Collection)

Photographed in March 2007 are the skeletal remains of the pier that before October 2005 held the sea-end railway station. (Marlinova Collection)

The attractive seating and lamps give an elegant feel to the very end of this most famous of piers, the longest pleasure pier in the world. *The Pier is Southend, Southend is the Pier.* (Marlinova Collection)

Opposite above: The *Sir William Heygate*, repainted in blue, at the sea-end railway station in March 2007. (Marlinova Collection)

Opposite below: The pier photographed from the stairs of the lifeboat station in March 2007. Note the absence of the demolished pavilion and the old pier head buildings where the surviving café building stands forlornly alone. (Marlinova Collection)

Other local titles published by Tempus

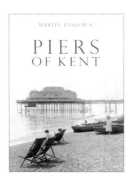

Piers of Kent

MARTIN EASDOWN

With its long coastline and mild climate, it was no surprise that Kent was at the forefront of the growth of the British seaside resort. From the 1860s a 'mania' developed amongst resorts to erect a showpiece pleasure pier. To cater for ever-increasing forms of entertainment, some piers were adapted to house ornate wooden pavilions, floral halls, theatres and amusements. With the majority of Kent's piers now only distant memories, this book will serve as a reminder of the county's golden pier age.

978-0-7524-4220-4

Essex Thame-Side Woolwich to Thorpe Bay

CHRIS THURMAN

Following on from his successful *London's River – Westminster to Woolwich*, Chris Thurman takes us on a further tour of the Thames from Woolwich to Thorpe Bay on the Essex side of the river. Much of the riverside is industrial, but this area is also home to many fishermen, day trippers and boating people as well as the many towns along the bank. From just beyond the futuristic sight of the Thames Barrier to sleepy Thorpe Bay, the changing landscape of Essex Thames-side is photographed over the past forty years in this stunning collection of images.

978-0-7524-3232-8

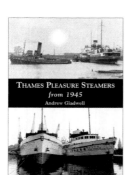

Thames Pleasure Steamers from 1945

ANDREW GLADWELL

To a generation of Londoners, the trip aboard a paddle steamer to the seaside was a traditional part of summer life. By the 1930s sleek new pleasure steamers were being introduced to gradually replace the older paddle steamers. By the late 1940s the stage was set for a new 'Golden Era' of the Thames pleasure steamer. People flocked from war-ravaged London and escaped down the water to Essex and Kent. Today preservation of the *Waverley*, *Balmoral* and *Kingswear Castle* have ensured that regular trips downriver have survived.

978-0-7524-2351-7

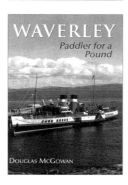

Waverley Paddler for a Pound

DOUGLAS MCGOWAN

Waverley, the world's last sea-going paddle steamer, was destined for the scrapyard in 1974 when Douglas McGowan and the Paddle Steamer Preservation Society purchased her for the princely sum of £1 and the rest is, as they say, history. Fresh from a £7 million refit in Great Yarmouth, *Waverley* is resplendent in her black, red and white livery and can be seen sailing the coast of Britain again.

978-0-7524-2877-2

If you are interested in purchasing other books published by Tempus, or in case you have difficulty finding any Tempus books in your local bookshop, you can also place orders directly through our website

www.tempus-publishing.com